Trends in Rare Books and Documents Special Collections Management, 2014-15 Edition

ISBN: 978-1-57440-297-1
Library of Congress Control Number: 2014946469

TABLE OF CONTENTS

DAVID M. RUBENSTEIN RARE BOOK & MANUSCRIPT LIBRARY, DUKE UNIVERSITY

We spoke with Dr. Naomi Nelson, Director of the David M. Rubenstein Rare Book & Manuscript Library at Duke University. Nelson has held this position at Rubenstein Library four years come August 2014.

General Description

Introduction

The David M. Rubenstein Rare Book & Manuscript Library is one of the largest special collections libraries in the Southeast. Its origins stretch back to the late 19th century, when a small rural college began to emphasize research over recitation. In the early 1890s, the school—then named Trinity College—began to acquire manuscript collections with a special focus on the southeastern United States. In 1942, upon receipt of the large and significant Trent Collection of Walt Whitman, the General Library established a Rare Books Department. Three decades later, the Duke University Archives was founded in 1972. Beginning in the 1990s, these collections were brought together as one and in 2006 were renamed the Rare Book, Manuscript, and Special Collections Library—later to become the David M. Rubenstein Rare Book & Manuscript Library.

As Duke University's home for special collections, managing more than 10,000 collections that include 375,000 volumes of rare books and over 20 million items in manuscript and archival collections, the Rubenstein Library is an academic and research hub not just for the Durham, North Carolina campus but on the global stage as well. "Researchers from around the world travel to Duke to see materials held nowhere else," boasts the library's website, and by the start of the 2015-16 academic school year, scholars will have even more reason to visit: the library's current transformative renovation is scheduled for completion summer 2015.

The Gift of David Rubenstein

In 2011, Duke alumnus and trustee David Rubenstein gifted an unprecedented $13.6 million to Duke University Libraries—the largest donation ever received by the Libraries—in support of the then-named Rare Book, Manuscript, and Special Collections Library. Duke's Board of Trustees quickly moved to rename the library in Rubenstein's honor, and Rubenstein's gift allowed the Duke Libraries to implement renovation plans that had begun more than a decade earlier. "We've gotten a lot of momentum from Mr. Rubenstein's gift," says Nelson. Construction officially began December 2012 as part of the final phase of the Perkins Project, prompting Rubenstein Library to move into its temporary home on the third floor of Perkins Library, the main branch of Duke's nine-branch library system in the center of West Campus. The building that will be the Rubenstein Library is located right next door—the original 1928 West Campus library building and its 1948 addition—where the library will eventually share space with the Duke University Libraries' administrative staff and Office of Business Services. "But the lion's share of the building will be devoted to Rubenstein [Library]," says Nelson.

What's in a Name

In its present state, Rubenstein Library exists as a collection of collections (10,000 strong). The Library is home to a trio of specialized research centers serving as its centerpiece—each center an established and focused collection in its own right—along with three newer collecting areas with dedicated staff and distinct identities. The library's new name has helped researchers and visitors to understand that these collections, along with many others, are all part of one library. "Becoming a named library gave us a sort of collective identity," says Nelson. "When I came to Duke and I talked to faculty, they knew about the particular collections they used in Special Collections, but they didn't have an awareness of the collection as a whole." Having a distinctive name for the library has been a boon for a collection as diverse as the Rubenstein's collection.

Collecting Strengths and the University Archives

Early collecting at Duke had established strong foundations in religious history, British and American literature, Southern history and literature, and the history of medicine. Notable collections from this time period include the Frank Baker Collection of Wesleyana and British Methodism and extensive collections of Southern plantation records.

More recently, the growing Human Rights Archive collects materials from grassroots organizations and transnational NGOs, religious and political leaders, human rights advocates, and artists. Significant history of medicine collections, first established in the Medical Center Library in 1931, moved to the Rare Book, Manuscript, and Special Collections Library in 2010. British and American Literature are particularly well represented in the Rubenstein, and the Economists' Papers Project—bringing together the papers of economists from across the country and around the world—covers the breadth of the 20th and 21st centuries. There is the unique Archive of Documentary Arts, host of the Full Frame Documentary Film Festival and home to the complete archives of many documentary photographers, from negatives to work prints to finished prints. The University Archives holds more than 11,000 linear feet of records dating from 1838 to the present.

"We have a traditional focus on literature and history," says Nelson, "but also a strong set of collections around social justice, [as well as] some more business-oriented collections like the history of economics and advertising."

The Research Centers

In time, the library also developed strengths away from the South. The library's collections had (and continue to have) a tight integration with research and teaching on campus, and from this mission statement emerged the opportunity to establish several new collecting strengths in responses to faculty interest and facilitated by donor support, establishing a trio of research centers in the 1990s that stand today as elite scholarly destinations in their respective fields.

The Sallie Bingham Center for Women's History and Culture, as described on the center's website, "acquires and preserves published and unpublished materials that reflect the public and private lives of women throughout history." What began first as an endowed archivist position in 1988 courtesy of author and female activist Sallie Bingham five years later grew into a permanently-endowed center (subsequently named in Bingham's honor in 1999). Relates Nelson: "We were asking ourselves, 'How can we build [a collection] that would be different than what else was out there?'" The Bingham Center houses a plethora of print, manuscript, and multimedia holdings, and is particularly known for its collections on women's reproductive health, second- and third-wave feminism, women and the arts and zines.

Around this same time Bingham first endowed the women's studies archivist position, the Rare Book, Manuscript, and Special Collections Library acquired the J. Walter Thompson Company (JWT) Archives, the most comprehensive historical record of any advertising agency. Duke was quick to build around this hefty collection, and in 1992, with the support of Duke alumnus John W. Hartman, the library created the John W. Hartman Center for Sales, Advertising & Marketing History. "It's the largest advertising collection of its kind," says Nelson, "and includes a wide variety of advertising formats." For example, while collection strengths already included and a host of agency and collector records, the center just added collections in outdoor advertising and direct marketing. In all, the Hartman Center holds more than 3 million items.

The last of these three centers came into being in 1995, when historian and scholar Dr. John Hope Franklin donated his professional and personal papers to the library, thus establishing the John Hope Franklin Research Center for African and American History and Culture. The center "collects, preserves, and promotes the use of published and unpublished primary sources for the exploration, understanding, and advancement of scholarship of the history and culture of Africa and the people of the African Diaspora in the Americas," with holdings from the slavery era as well as 21st century materials. With particular strengths in African American intellectuals, the slave family, the Jim Crow South, Civil Rights, and African American experiences of Africa, the Franklin Research Center is an authority on the history and culture of Africa and people of African descent in the Americas.

Acquisitions and Development

Growing Operations

The Rubenstein Library manages 20 endowments and has access to funds from several Duke University Libraries collection endowments in addition. Nelson estimates that about 75 percent of Rubenstein Library's collection funding stems from endowments and restricted funds, with 23 percent coming from the library budget and the last two percent stemming from gifts and grants. While the restrictive funds can be quite specific ("We have one fund that's for American humor," adds Nelson, "and another for early Greek liturgical manuscripts"), there is room to allocate funds to support a range of collecting areas.

"A lot of the collections we've gotten over time have been gifts," Nelson continues, citing that about 75 percent of manuscript acquisitions and about 73 percent of print acquisitions are gifts. For example, just last year Rubenstein Library acquired about 1,010 print titles and 1,300 linear feet of materials through gifts.

"As our collections grow, our services and programs need to keep pace," says Nelson. "We have added staff in every area: collection development, technical services, and research services." Rubenstein Library consists of 27 permanent professional librarians and seven non-exempt staff, as well as eight graduate interns selected from the four Research Triangle area universities. "For many years we have focused most of our development efforts on capital projects, such as the renovation, and on providing support for staffing and programming. Our goal for the next five years is to significantly increase [our] collection endowments."

Security and Theft

Increased Security with the Renovation

As with all diligent rare book libraries, Rubenstein Library is cognizant of and responsive to issues of security and theft, and "like any major special collections," Rubenstein Library has been made a target in the past. "[Gilbert] Bland visited us," says Nelson, "[Stephen] Blumberg visited us," referring to two of history's most notorious rare book thieves. As such, security and theft is something the library continues to think about. "We were in a building that was last renovated in the 1960s, and technology has changed since then." With the renovation, Nelson says Rubenstein Library is taking the opportunity to revamp their security policies. "We've established different security zones," she says, "with integrated digital video security systems. We're much more integrated with Perkins Library security as well as with Duke University Police," noting that Perkins Library is also getting a new security officer.

Digitization

Early Adopters

Duke was one of the early libraries to create a digitization program in the 1990s, and with more than 200,000 items available online and about 3.5 million page views per year, the university has established an impressive body of digital work. At the direction of Digital Projects and Production Services (part of the Duke University Libraries' Information Technology Services Division), much of this digitization work is internally funded. What's more, Nelson estimates that about 95 percent of the items in the digital collection are drawn from Rubenstein Library, with the expressed goal of highlighting collection strengths. "We also have a number of projects that directly support faculty teaching," says Nelson, citing one such project in which a class is developing an innovative viewer designed especially for using digital versions of anatomical flap-books. The library also looks to digitize materials that are very hard to use in their original form (such as glass negatives) as well as materials related to Duke's history.

Most digitization work for Rubenstein Library is completed in-house. The few projects that are outsourced are done so either due to time constraints or else due to format issues. "We also will digitize small amounts of materials on demand," Nelson says, although she relates that they don't yet get a lot of requests for digitization from faculty related to classroom use. Duke has also been an early adopter of MOOCs (Massive Open Online Courses), and in the future this may raise a challenge in balancing staff time and resources between on-site and virtual instruction. "It takes a certain amount of time to prepare for classes coming on-site, and a different kind of effort [to meet the needs of online classes]." Muses Nelson, "Is this an expansion of our overall mission?"

Outreach and Publicity

Online Presence and Social Media

The Rubenstein Library has made a considerable effort to cultivate an active online presence. In addition to a multi-faceted and extensive website (http://library.duke.edu/rubenstein), the library maintains *The Devil's Tale* (http://blogs.library.duke.edu/rubenstein), the library's blog five-and-a-half years running now. "The blog is very successful," explains Nelson. "It talks about collections and services and upcoming events. It's a great place to find out what's happening at Rubenstein." In addition to these pages, the library maintains several Facebook pages (including some for each individual research center), as well as a

Twitter account and a Flickr stream. A subcommittee at Rubenstein is tasked with managing the library's social media presence.

Public Relations and Outreach

There also exists a public relations team within Rubenstein Library, as well as a Communications Director for the Duke University Libraries as a whole. "We also get great support from the Office of News and Communications." A lot of blog posts that first appear on *The Devil's Tale* have been subsequently picked up by local and national media outlets alike (Duke Today, the news and information portal for the Duke University community, has been particularly supportive in this respect). One particular series of posts, exploring the period-specific advertising threads found in the HBO series *Mad Men*, are quite popular and get picked up often. Rubenstein Library also has the two-year-old *RL Magazine* at its disposal: "It's a beautiful publication we can hand to donors. It helps people understand our collections and our programs."

Events and Exhibits

Events

In addition to online outreach, Rubenstein Library supports a robust event schedule, putting on about 50 events each year. "Film screenings, panel discussions, book readings," Nelson rattles off. "They can be small or large gatherings, up to 200 people. A lot of events are joint efforts with faculty, and we do a lot of co-sponsoring." Among the highlights on the calendar is the annual reception for the WOLA-Duke Book Award for honoring the best current, non-fiction book published in English on human rights, democracy, and social justice in contemporary Latin America. Or there's the Honickman First Book Prize in Photography, awarded every other year to a North American photographer that "uses his or her camera for creative exploration, whether it be of places, people, or communities; of the natural or social world; of beauty at large or the lack of it; of objective or subjective realities." The Barbaralee Diamonstein-Spielvogel Visiting Filmmaker Series brings a filmmaker to campus "to address significant contemporary topics of social, political, economic, and cultural urgency from a global perspective" (a complementary visiting artist program also brings artists to campus for four weeks in the fall). The Sallie Bingham Center, too, hosts a symposium every three or four years, while on a smaller scale the Archive of Documentary Arts and Human Rights Archive co-sponsor the *Rights! Camera! Action!* human rights documentary screening series.

Exhibits and Exhibition Space

"We don't do hiatuses here at Duke," jokes Nelson, and while the current renovation to the library has slowed Rubenstein Library's exhibition schedule, reducing the library to just one exhibition space, the solution is simply to look for other spaces in the meantime. The renovation will more than double the library's exhibition space, and Nelson says the library will have three or four exhibits annually, as well as the ability to display materials that have just come in. "Duke has a renewed emphasis on student research and scholarship," and this plays a key role in dictating exhibition schedules. Past popular exhibits put on by Rubenstein Library have included an *Animated Anatomies* exhibit, featuring materials from the History of Medicine Collection as well as materials on loan from the University of Padua. Nelson recalls "Mapping the City: A Stranger's Guide," a cartographic exhibit curated by students from the Borderworks Humanities Lab. More recently, an exhibition from the Sidney Gamble collection of photographs of early 20th century China has been touring China and will culminate with the grand opening of the university's China campus—Duke Kunshan University—in the fall of 2014.

Rubenstein Library is also growing in its practice of lending materials. "We are getting increasing numbers of requests to loan materials," reports Nelson, "especially for photographs from the Archives of Documentary Arts." Rubenstein loans materials about five to seven times each year, but, as Nelson says, "it takes a lot of effort to do that well," involving coordination across several departments and institutions. "We would like to grow this capacity over time, including additional staffing." With renovations near completion, that time is near.

SPECIAL COLLECTIONS, UNIVERSITY OF GLASGOW

We spoke with Julie Gardham, Senior Librarian and Manager of Special Collections at the University of Glasgow. Gardham has been with Special Collections for 17 years, the last two as Manager.

General Description

Five Hundred Years and Counting

The story of Special Collections at the University of Glasgow is as old as the university itself—no small claim considering the Scottish university's rich and extensive history. Founded in 1451, the University of Glasgow stands as the fourth-oldest university in the English-speaking world. It is one of the British Isles' seven ancient universities, and since its foundation the University has housed a library, although it wasn't until the 1960s that Special Collections came together as a designated unit. "So what we have," explains Gardham, "is an accumulation of collections spanning five hundred years."

"At that point," says Gardham, referring to the founding of Special Collections, "there was a need to have a designated person in charge." It all came to a head in 1968, when the University of Glasgow Library moved into a new building on campus and Special Collections officially came together, organizing more than five centuries' worth of rare book and manuscript collecting at the University, first in the Library's basement, then in a custom-built department on the top floor of the 12-story building. The floor, which was built as an addition on the Library's roof in 1997, features an environmentally-controlled book stack, seminar room, and reading room.

Wide Subject Coverage

With more than 500 years of collecting experience, subject coverage for Special Collections is understandably wide. "It's across the board. A lot of literature, a lot of history of medicine, history of science, art, theology." The collections amass more than 200,000 printed items, many of which are pre-18th century, including over 1,000 incunabula (items printed before 1501). Special Collections also boasts between 200,000 and 300,000 manuscript items. The holdings span more than 2,000 years of human activity, from the first to the 21st century, establishing Special Collections at the University of Glasgow as an internationally significant collection and one of the foremost resources for academic research and teaching in Scotland and beyond.

The Hunterian Collection

The most notable of the Library's rare book collections is the Hunterian Collection. Assembled by Scottish anatomist and physician Dr. William Hunter in the 18th century, the collection includes over 10,000 printed books and 650 manuscripts from Hunter's personal library, with over 500 incunabula, a large assortment of medieval manuscripts (including the Hunterian Psalter, an illuminated manuscript from the 12th century), and scores of working papers detailing Hunter's work in anatomy and medicine. In addition to the host of medicine books, the collection, which came to the University in 1807, also showcases Hunter's interests in topography, numismatics, fine art, astronomy, botany, zoology, and travel, among other topics. The holdings of Special Collections are further complemented by collections at the Hunterian Museum and Art Gallery, also located on campus, which previously held the entire collection until much of it was taken into the care of the Library in the 20th century. "The creation of Special Collections was the final process after a long line of collecting," Gardham says of Hunter, who died in 1783.

Additional Collecting Strengths

Special Collections claims an array of collecting strengths outside the Hunterian Library as well. The Euing Collection, acquired by the University via donation in the 19th century, brings together the library of William Euing (1788-1874), a Glasgow insurance broker. The collection contains about 7,000 printed books and volumes (including a copy of the Shakespeare First Folio), 3,000 bibles, psalters, and books of prayers and hymns (with editions dating as far back as the 15th century), and 2,500 volumes of early printed music (including two medieval liturgical works, an early 17th century lute book, and biographical documents and letters to John Sainsbury for use in *A Dictionary for Musicians* (1824)).

The Murray Collection, which also came to the University by way of donation, contains over 15,000 printed books from the personal library of David Murray, 19th century Glasgow lawyer, antiquarian, and bibliographer, presenting a superb regional history (particularly the West of Scotland) with items dating as far back as the 15th century. The Ferguson Collection gathers the library of John Ferguson (1838-1916), Professor of Chemistry at the University of Glasgow for over four decades. Acquired in 1921, the 7,500 volumes in this collection are particularly focused on alchemy and chemistry and constitute one of the world's best on the subject. "[The Ferguson Collection] attracts scholars from all over the world," says Gardham.

Also a major draw for scholars near and far is the Stirling Maxwell Collection: containing nearly 2,000 volumes, the collection showcases Sir Stirling Mawell's unrivaled collection of emblem and device literature, with texts ranging in origin from the 16th century to the 19th century. Bequeathed to the Library in 1956, the collection stands as one of the best in the world, with . The Library seeks to grow the collection whenever possible. Notes Gardham: "[Emblem books] are actively researched at the University." Further information regarding the University's ongoing research can be found here, at the Stirling Maxwell Centre: http://www.gla.ac.uk/schools/mlc/research/thestirlingmaxwellcentre.

Other notable collections include the Hill & Adamson Collection, which includes the early work of 19th century Scottish photographers David Octavius Hill and Robert Adamson, as well as the correspondences (about 7,000 letters) of artist James McNeill Whistler, "a collection of international importance" as Gardham calls it. The Scottish Theater Archive is a consistently expanding collection popular with students, faculty, and the general theater public alike, and as with the Stirling Maxwell Collection, the Library is actively adding to the Archive.

The University Archive

Separate from Special Collections, and housed in a separate building entirely, the University Archive collects the official records of the University created and accumulated since its foundation in 1451. Remarks Gardham: "For most university libraries, these two departments, which have all these heritage materials, would be merged. But we're still separate." The main obstacle in merging the two units is space. "We can't build any more floors on top of [the library]!" jokes Gardham. But while the Archive, which also maintains a substantial business archive, has been housed in a separate building (with its own reading room) on the opposite side of the campus for the past ten years, there is some promise that developments on campus within the next decade will provide an opportunity to bring the two units together: the University owns the land currently occupied by a hospital that has plans to move in the future. "At some point then," Gardham predicts, "there will be a scope to merge."

Staff

Special Collections employs 12 paid members of staff, although not all members are full-time. "Some are very part-time," says Gardham. "We also have three part-time honorary librarians who are basically former members of staff. They're kind of volunteering now." Special Collections also hosts student work placements throughout the year. "These are for specific courses, undergrad and post-grad, and can go on for several weeks or even months." In this capacity, students are assigned a project, usually in place of a dissertation, and are often tasked with creating displays and completing vital cataloging work. "This is a growing area for us," explains Gardham of student work placement. "The University is very keen on this." At present, Special Collections can take on no more than three or four students at one time, although this is likely to expand in the future. "It's a question of having enough staff to supervise," says Gardham, "as well as having enough space."

Acquisitions and Development

Acquisitions on a Budget

"Because money is quite tight, we have to be strict," Gardham says of the collection development policy at Special Collections. To put it another way: "For purchases, we're very limited." While Special Collections does have three endowments at its disposal, these are a set amount each year, and Gardham admits these three do "not have much money in them." The first of the endowments allows for the most freedom and can be spent on any aspect of the collection. "We do have targeted collections we focus on, such as the anatomical texts and the Hunterian Collection." The second endowment is used specifically for the development of Scottish imprints in the Murray Collection, while the third is stipulated for acquisitions in the Scottish Theater Archive. "We supplement the funds available by applying to national bodies, such as the National Fund for Acquisitions. They will provide matching funds, so we apply to them two or three times a year for purchases." The University of Glasgow Library also has a Friends of the Library group, which Gardham relates also assists with acquisition funds. "For most purchases," says Gardham, "we will seek matching funds from one of these two groups." In all, Gardham estimates Special Collections acquires through purchase six or seven items a year.

Additional Support and Donations

With available funds at a premium, Special Collections must also look for support elsewhere in most effectively applying its acquisition and collection development efforts. In this light, also at Gardham's disposal is the Rare Books in Scotland (RBiS), a forum facilitated by the National Library of Scotland for members of staff in Scottish libraries and other organizations who have responsibility for collections of rare books. "We meet one or two times a year and we share our collection development policies," says Gardham of the network of rare book librarians. "So if something comes up for sale, we can alert one another. It's a way to try and collaborate on acquisitions." The network and its librarians act as extra pairs of eyes and ears in the hunt for acquisitions.

Donations also provide a source for acquisitions for Special Collections, although not always a consistent source. As Gardham reports, donations come in "sometimes thick and fast, sometimes not at all," and they tend to be offers of archival-type donations. "Usually people's papers," she says, and not so often books. "We don't have the staff to deal with a lot coming in, so sometimes we have to turn donations down. Sometimes they are looking to donate something we already have. We will only take things if they do fit in with our collection development policy."

Digitization

Appetite for Digitization

While Gardham acknowledges that Special Collections has "very little which is digitized in its entirety," she notes that there is a "real appetite for [digitization], and [we're] very much aware of that." A photographic department that is part of the University Library maintains a dedicated team, and while "the technology's there," there are only three full-time photographers in the department, just one of which is assigned to photographing books. With this department servicing the entire university (they also complete digitization work for the Hunterian Museum and the University Archive, for example), staff resources can stretch understandably thin. Although Gardham notes, "if there's specific project work to be done, they can bring in extra staff to deal with it." The end-goal is to be digitizing whole books in their entirety.

Open Access

"Our problem at the moment," explains Gardham, "is that we do have thousands of images on file from various books and manuscripts. But these images aren't publicly accessible yet. We don't have an image management system." The good news is that Special Collections has recently purchased KE Software's Electronic Museum management system (EMu), the same management system that's already being used on campus at the Hunterian Museum. The system will allow the library to manage not just single images but entire collections at a time. Jokes Gardham, "I hear it's going to be the answer to all our prayers."

Concerning the materials Special Collections looks to digitize, the number one priority is to support teaching and research at the university. "We want to get away from being restrictive and to make it openly accessible." At the moment, Special Collections has a long-running project to catalog and detail the incunabula. A sample of four or five images from each book has been gathered in a massive Flickr set totaling more than 3,000 images ("We can't digitize them all in their entirety"). The Library also can digitize on demand, and maintains a copy of each file that is digitized. "So we've got a large bank of images. It's just a question of making them publicly available."

Outreach and Publicity

An Active Online Presence

When asked if Special Collections maintains an active online presence, Gardham's quick response is spirited and resolute: "Absolutely!" The collection's website (www.gla.ac.uk/services/specialcollections) is a multifaceted portal with a wealth of information, with sections to support various courses, a large virtual exhibition section, and links to the aforementioned Flickr set. "We've been adding to it for years and years," explains Gardham of the website. "We've been blogging for several years," she adds, "and we aim for two to three new blog posts each week. These could be anything from news about recent acquisitions to inquiries we've received about our materials." Special Collections also maintains a dedicated Twitter account (now a year old), which Gardham reports has allowed them to reach out to new audiences. In addition to these outlets, Special Collections benefits from the University Library's official Facebook profile, as well an Instagram account, often feeding posts and updates to library staff to disseminate through these channels. "We're trying to be as wide-ranging as possible with social media. We're very open with that."

Exhibits and Events

Isolation on the Twelfth Floor

The downside of making a home on Level 12 of a 12-story building is the increased isolation from the general public. "We can't just rely on people coming up to the twelfth floor," says Gardham. "So we have to go to the people." Compounding this problem is the limited amount of exhibition space available to Special Collections. "[Acquiring additional exhibition space] is something that's always talked about. And that might happen, but it's not in the works at the moment." Special Collections currently controls a small showcase in the foyer on Level 12, which Gardham says is used to highlight collections. "We turn this around three or four times a year." They also have a case in the Hunterian Museum and Art Gallery, a publicly accessible museum, rotating display items throughout the year. "The only other exhibition space we have is when we sometimes arrange with the Hunterian Museum to do a book exhibition, but this happens only every five or ten years." At present, Special Collections is planning such an exhibition, a large collection of incunabula in the Art Gallery section of the museum. Showcasing approximately 60 books, the display will open in February 2015 and stay on display until June. "Because we're on the twelfth floor," says Gardham, "there isn't a kind of space where you can just wander in. You need a card to get in. Anyone can come up and use Special Collections and use the reading room, but it's a bit of a barrier. Sometimes it feels like we're not open to the public, yet we are.

"That's why we try to focus on putting so much online," she continues, "because we don't have a lot of physical space." Likewise, Special Collections has a pop-up display that can be used for temporary exhibits and events when the need arises. The collections also entertain a high demand for lending requests: "If the conditions are right, we will loan," says Gardham, estimating that Special Collections makes about four or five loans each year. "At the moment, we've got six alchemy manuscripts in Düsseldorf, Germany. We've also got some [James McNeill] Whistler items going out to Japan later in the year, as well as some William Blake prints that will be going to a big exhibition in Oxford in November. We're quite happy to loan materials to external exhibitions."

Special Collections recently hosted what Gardham calls "research opportunities," an evening at the library highlighting underused areas of the collection, replete with wine and food. "The idea is to get university people in and to get them to look at the materials." Special Collections also puts on show-and-tell sessions for interested groups—not just academic groups, but for historical societies and the like as well. "We will give talks," explains Gardham. "The Scottish Theater Archive is a popular one. We are keen to do more public-type events, not just focusing on the academic population but engaging the public as a whole as well."

Security and Theft

No Major Threats

While life on the twelfth floor can render the stacks in Special Collections somewhat lonely and inaccessible, the upside is obvious from a security standpoint: "The feeling on the twelfth floor is a little isolated, but it's also a bit of a stronghold." Gardham reports that Special Collections has not experienced any major thefts, and while the collections are only open until 6 p.m. each day, the premises are alarmed twenty-four hours a day, accompanied by a presence of security guards. The twelfth floor features a supervised reading room in which, during open hours, a member of staff is always on duty, as well as closed-circuit televisions in both the reading room and public spaces such as the foyer and corridor. Although it's not a pressing concern, "[theft] is something we're aware of and we try not to forget about it." As such, there will always be at least two members of staff on duty, and visitors are required to sign-in with photo identification. "Everywhere is highly visible," Gardham says of their space on the twelfth floor.

Looking Ahead

Attracting Patrons

"It's a great collection, and it gets a lot of use," says Gardham. But she is always looking for increased exposure and increased interaction with the public. "The more the merrier—and if we could extend it even more," she hopes. "I suppose it's like most special collections: no matter how welcoming you are, no matter how active on Twitter you are, it's still hard to overcome. It's a great resource, and the University of Glasgow is lucky to have [Special Collections]. But sometimes it's easy to forget that we're here and for use. Especially with undergraduates. We're always exploring ways to draw undergraduates in." One such promotion was a blog-a-thon hosted by Special Collections. Students were invited to submit blog posts—about a collection or even simply one book—to compete for one of two cash prizes. "If you can get them as undergrads, then they might go on to post-grad work, research work, etcetera. We try to be accessible to anyone. We have very few restrictions on the books and manuscripts. We'll welcome anyone."

SPECIAL COLLECTIONS, BRYN MAWR COLLEGE

We spoke with Eric Pumroy, Associate Chief Information Officer and Seymour Adelman Head of Special Collections. Pumroy has served as head of the collection since 1999.

General Description

Bringing It All Together

Bryn Mawr College was founded in 1885, and for over 125 years the women's liberal arts college located ten miles outside Philadelphia has been a bastion for women's rights, equality, and education. Special Collections at Bryn Mawr explores these issues prominently, with predictably strong holdings in women's history—although also collected here are standout holdings in early modern books, travel accounts, and the study of antiquity, as well as one of the largest academic collections of 15th century printed books in the country. "[Bryn Mawr] is a little unusual," says Pumroy, "in that the college doesn't have a museum. So Special Collections is not just rare books and manuscripts. It holds the College's art and artifact collections as well." As such, Special Collections can be roughly divided into two broad collection areas: 1) Rare Books, Manuscripts, and Archives, and 2) Art and Artifact Collections.

On the Rare Books, Manuscripts, and Archives side, the collection boasts roughly 50,000 rare books, with manuscripts spanning 2,000 linear feet. "These are mostly things that relate to women's history, particularly people associated with college." Showcased here are the papers of Katharine Sergeant White: fiction editor of *The New Yorker* for more than 30 years, wife of E.B. White, and Bryn Mawr alum. The women's rights movement is extensively covered, highlighted by the papers of educator and suffragist Carey Thomas, second President of the College and one of the first women college presidents.

On the Art and Artifact Collections side—sometimes called College's Collections—are more than 50,000 objects gathered under five main collecting strengths: fine art (including between 10,000 and 15,000 prints, drawings, and photographs, from early modern through the 20th century), archaeology, anthropology, decorative arts, and geology. "These are really teaching collections," Pumroy says, for the benefit of Bryn Mawr faculty, students, and outside scholars alike, adding that items in the Art and Artifact Collections do get exhibited periodically as well, both at Bryn Mawr and as loans to museums. These collections have developed nearly since Bryn Mawr's foundation, first as a series of departmental collections and then as a more cohesive unit since the 1980s. Included here are Native American artifacts such as Peruvian textiles and pre-Colombian items, African art and Chinese, Japanese, and Korean scrolls and other art works. The archaeology collection in particular includes artifacts such as coins and glasswork from Greece and Rome, an asset to what is one of the oldest independent archaeology departments in the country—Bryn Mawr has offered PhD programs in archaeology since the beginning of the 20th century, and while on the undergraduate level the college remains women-only, the college has since accepted men into its graduate programs.

Increased Visibility

"Administratively, [Rare Books, Manuscripts, and Archives and Art and Artifact Collections] have been united for quite a while now," although Special Collections staff and collections were only physically merged four years ago when a renovated and expanded Special Collections space opened in the main library building. The renovations both increased the visibility of all of the collections and enabled the program to operate in a more coordinator manner.

Special Collections and its staff of about eight are all housed on the second floor of the Mariam Coffin Canaday Library, the college's main library. Many of the collections are now housed in Canady Library, although important parts are still housed in other buildings on campus, reports Pumroy. The recently-renovated second floor features a first-rate, modern reading room, a seminar room for teaching, and space for work and storage. Pumroy adds that in addition to the eight staff members, Special Collections is home to a host of student workers (both undergraduate and graduate) who are paid for by a combination of funds from the department, academic programs, and gifts and grants in support of special projects.

Acquisitions and Development

Acquisitions Process

The acquisitions process for Special Collections is a multi-part structure. Reporting to Pumroy are the individual curators, one each for Rare Books, Manuscripts, and Archives and for Art and Artifact Collections. "They do a fair amount of the legwork," says Pumroy, which includes liaising with donors. There is also a collections committee consisting of faculty, administrators in the alumni and development office, and board members. "It a collection gets to a particular size or value, then the acquisition has to be approved by the committee," he explains.

Special Collections does have an acquisitions budget, which Pumroy explains is primarily for rare books. "It helps that our acquisition money was endowed," he says, "that it wasn't a line item that could be cut." But space is limited in the library. "Because we've been so tight on space, we haven't been able to be aggressive [with acquisitions]. Even one significant collection is quite noticeable, and it changes the way we think about our responsibilities for the next few years." As such, Special Collections acquires, through purchase, about 100 books per year, books that range in value from a simple $10 piece of ephemera to a $12,000 early modern museum catalog. Donations, on the other hand, tend to fluctuate. "Two years ago, we got a quite significant collection of twentieth century art prints, about seven or eight hundred pieces. But this year, there was no major collection like that." Pumroy says manuscript collections tend to come in via donation, with Special Collections acquiring about 50 linear feet this year.

Grants

Pumroy reports that Special Collections has benefited from several grants over the years. "At any given time," he says, "we probably have about $20,000 in various donor-restricted funds. We just finished off one grant project, [establishing] the Albert M. Greenfield Digital Center for the History of Women's Education." The $300,000 grant, courtesy of the Philadelphia-based Albert M. Greenfield Foundation, created the Center as a digital hub "to foster inquiry and dialogue on how the history of women's education has informed contemporary life and how it will shape the global future." Pumroy also points out a recently awarded grant from the National Endowment for the Humanities (NEH), one he describes as "a little more complicated" as it is a joint project with Bryn Mawr's fellow Seven Sisters colleges. "We're trying to figure out a way to make it easy for students and scholars to get to our digital collections of student letters and diaries in a single search."

Digitization

A Shared Catalog

Digitization efforts at Bryn Mawr "started in a pretty serious way about ten years ago," when a shared online digital catalog was created with Haverford and Swarthmore Colleges (together the three schools constitute the Tri-College Consortium). The online catalog, known as Triptych (http://triptych.brynmawredu/cdm), compiles and shares all the library collection systems across the three institutions. "We all got together and acquired CONTENTdm," the digital collection management software from OCLC, which remains in use at Bryn Mawr to this day. Of course, in the past ten years, many more systems have emerged, such as a system for art and artifacts, or an institutional repository where the library can place larger scale documents, such as college publications.

Concerning what materials gets digitized, then, Pumroy relates that what Bryn Mawr was doing at first was "very targeted and modest." But Special Collections quickly began taking projects on a systematic basis. This included the digitization of art and artifacts, historical photographs, alumni magazines, course catalogs, yearbooks, and literary magazines.

While Special Collections does not have a dedicated digitization staff, Bryn Mawr's Visual Resources Department completes a certain amount of scanning for them, although "for some of the bigger projects," says Pumroy, "we send those out," as part of a program for mass digitization. "We did have some funding, so we were able to digitize seventy-five years of course catalogs, without having to spend much staff time on it." There are also smaller projects that are done in response to individual needs, meeting the requests of both faculty and outside scholars. "But our major priority for the next few years is working on documentation on the history of the college, particularly the experiences of women students."

Outreach and Publicity

A Major Reorganization

Bryn Mawr College is moving its website to a content management system, Drupal, and with that there is a major reorganization on the horizon for the Special Collections website. "The goal is to think about it from a user's point of view," says Pumroy. "What do [users] want to know when they come to the website, and how do they get to where they need to get to as efficiently as possible?" Pumroy explains that the collection's website now is mostly departmental-driven, not user-driven, and as such the reorganization looks to place the website within the context of the teaching, learning, and research initiatve.

Social Media

"Social media has become huge," says Pumroy, and Special Collections has been diligent in keeping up with a changing public relations landscape. The Canaday Library has a Facebook profile, as does Bryn Mawr's Friends of the Library group and the Greenfield Digital Center (in addition to several Tumblr sites). "It's become a huge part of the college's outreach. So the more we do using our blogs, Facebook, Tumblr, then the more it gets picked up by the college as a whole." Pumroy points out that responsibilities for handling social media at Special Collections is spread around among all the staff members.

Exhibits

Creating a Permanent Exhibition Space

When Canady Library opened in 1970, it included a Rare Book Room on the main floor, which doubled as both a reading room and exhibition space. Over the last decade, it has gradually been converted to the College's main exhibition space, with the use of movable walls to transform this panelled room into a space which Special Collections uses to show both books and contemporary art from the collection. In all, Special Collections has at its disposal the main gallery space on the first floor as well as some satellite spaces on the second floor, including a large exhibition space across from the reading room. Around six exhibitions are scheduled for any given year, and Pumroy reports that Special Collections is operating on a year-and-a-half schedule.

Education as a Top Priority

At present, Special Collections is wrapping up a student-curated exhibit that has been on display for the entire spring semester, showcasing art in the 20th century, titled *A Century of Self-Expression: Modern American Art in the Collection of John and*

Joanne Payson. "An alumna who's an art collector of twentieth century modern American art was willing to lend us a fairly substantial part of her painting collection," says Pumroy. What the students in the two-semester class did, under the direction of the curator of art and a senior member of the art history department, was put together a show that focuses on the development of art coming out of the 1913 International Exhibition of Modern Art in New York City, more popularly known as the legendary Armory Show. "The students wrote exhibition text, catalog text—everything including figuring out what should hang where." Pumroy tells of another student-curated exhibit a few years ago on medieval art, in which students had also shouldered the responsibility of writing the text, deciding how to display the items, and other such organizational duties that go into putting on an exhibit. "[A student-curated exhibit] gets to the larger issue of what our priorities are: the educational experience of the students."

Pumroy continues: "The reason we have these things is not to preserve them in some general way, or even to make them available for research for the scholarly world. At a liberal arts college, our primary reason for existence is the education of our students." He adds that Special Collections usually complements the physical exhibition with a web version as well.

Security and Theft

A Secure Collection

While theft has never been an alarming concern, Pumroy reports that nonetheless it is something of which Special Collections is acutely aware. "We've taken steps [to ensure security]. Everything's locked. There are security cameras and security systems. Patrons can't use something from the collection without staff there." He also reports that staff looks at its security measures periodically. For instance, Special Collections is currently undergoing a larger study of collection storage, as everything is and always has been held on campus.

Collaboration

The Tri-College Consortium

Special Collections at Bryn Mawr goes beyond just the holdings and resources available in Canaday Library. Pumroy emphasizes the benefits of a strong collaboration between the three schools in the Tri-College Consortium (Bryn Mawr, Haverford, and Swarthmore). "Because we share a single catalog, there's a lot of cross registration between the colleges," says Pumroy, "especially between Haverford and Bryn Mawr." The strength of Haverford's collection, for example—located just a mile from Bryn Mawr—is the history of American Quakers. "It's a very strong collection, and we don't have anything like that [at Bryn Mawr]. Our strength is a much broader collection of rare books on a wide range of subjects." As such, faculty from all three colleges utilize the shared materials often—sometimes a class from Haverford will come to Bryn Mawr, or vice versa, or else there is also the possibility of moving the materials themselves. "This makes it possible for all schools to have a broader range of collections to draw upon." The three colleges have even collaborated on joint exhibits in the past: "A few years ago we worked with Haverford on complementary exhibits on Charles Darwin."

PACSCL

Bryn Mawr College is also an active and founding member of the Philadelphia Area Consortium of Special Collections Libraries (PACSCL). The organization, now in its 30th year, is a far-reaching collaboration of 36 area institutions, including the University of Pennsylvania, Temple University, a host of smaller liberal arts colleges, independent research institutions, and historical societies alike. According to its website, "[PACSCL] was born out of the conviction that the extraordinary collections of Philadelphia area libraries deserved greater visibility and broader support." Says Pumroy: "One of the things we've realized is that technology becomes more and more important for institutions to be visible. You have to have a significantly technology capability to be a player in the research world." The challenge, of course, is adapting to rapid changes in technology, requiring both extensive resources and technical expertise.

"Being able to collaborate on digital projects really opens up a lot of opportunities to keep costs under control," Pumroy continues, "to be able to undertake more and more ambitious projects." A shared database of finding aids has been established, currently hosted at the University of Pennsylvania, and Special Collections at Bryn Mawr is in the process of converting its finding aids to mount onto the PACSCL site ("We're not yet there, but we're moving down that road," says Pumroy). "We're also starting to talk about building similar capabilities for hosting digital collections," says Pumroy. PACSCL's first wave of digital projects in the 1990s and 2000s were powered by some large processing and cataloging grants. At the time, the aim was to digitize those materials which highlighted and showcased their collections. "But now we can say, 'What's the purpose of doing this?' We can do something that's a little more curated. It's not a question of *who* owns the materials, but rather how can we bring these materials together to make the collection better with multiple institutions." The goal now, Pumroy explains, is to be able to go to one site where patrons can search across all the collections instantaneously.

UNIVERSITY ARCHIVES & SPECIAL COLLECTIONS, UNIVERSITY OF SASKATCHEWAN

We spoke with Tim Hutchinson, Head of University Archives & Special Collections. Prior to being named Head this past year, Hutchinson had served as University Archivist since 2004.

General Description

Coming Together

For years the Special Collections and University Archives units at the University of Saskatchewan have shared space in the main library on the U of S main campus. It was not until July 2013, however, that the merged department of University Archives & Special Collections was established within the University Library. Still located in Murray Library, which the collections have called home since 1974 when construction completed on the library's new southern wing (the building itself opened in 1956), University Archives & Special Collections (UASC) has an informal history that nearly dates to the university's foundation in 1907. "The first University Archivist was hired in 1970," relates Hutchinson. "But even well before that, Arthur Morton, the first University Librarian [appointed in 1914], was gathering records." By 1917, students in the historical association were being enlisted in a project to preserve material relating to the history of the prairies, and by 1930 Morton could claim the largest body of material outside of the Archives in Ottawa on the history of the prairie provinces.

University Archives

"The University of Saskatchewan has long had a role to document and research the province [of Saskatchewan]," Hutchinson continues, and with a strong focus on university records and people related to the institution, University Archives has been doing just that. "In terms of documenting university history, we do quite well compared to other universities in Canada. We have both institutional records and faculty records," as well as records of organizations related to the university, such as student organizations. As one of the few professionally-run archives in the province, University Archives & Special Collections boasts over 4,500 linear meters of materials (primarily acquired by University Archives, but including archival materials from Special Collections). Among these materials are the papers and records of the Saskatchewan Wheat Pool, a grain handling, agri-food processing, and marketing company (and former cooperative, later renamed Viterra). The Wheat Pool collection, donated to the Archives in 2001, gathered over 6,700 slides and 2,600 photographs detailing the farming landscape of the prairie province. "These grain elevators used to be all over," explains Hutchinson. Since this initial donation, over 40,000 slides and transparencies have been added in a recent accrual, particularly documenting more recent years. In all, the images in the collection—as well as extensive textual records—seek to illustrate the strong social, economic, and political roles the company played in Saskatchewan.

In addition to the Saskatchewan Wheat Pool collection, University Archives compiles a good number of photographic sets, such as the recently-acquired Courtney Milne collection, showcasing over half a million slides and digital images of the late Canadian photographer's work. Milne, a U of S alum, took hundreds of thousands of photographs on all seven continents, and his entire personal collection is gathered in this massive donation. Fellow U of S alum Henry Taube is the subject of another recent acquisition, collecting the medals, awards, plaques, and certificates (as well as textual materials and photographs) of the first Canadian-born Nobel Prize winner in Chemistry. Among the materials in this collection is Taube's 1983 Nobel Prize itself—Taube remains the only U of S graduate ever to receive the award.

Special Collections

On the other side of the coin is the print collection from Special Collections. Rare book collecting at the University of Saskatchewan has been built up over many years, the basis of which was Arthur Morton's initial prairie collection, coupled with the acquisition of a collection of materials now known as the Adam Shortt Library of Canadiana. Shortt, a political economist from Ontario in the late 19th and early 20th centuries, had compiled a set of old and rare materials exploring the history of western Canada. Additions are made to the Shortt collection regularly, which now contains approximately 50,000 volumes.

More recently, Special Collections was gifted a large donation from Erasmus scholar and U of S Professor Emeritus Peter Bietenholz. The Bietenholz Rare Book Collection is a "significant compilation of books in a number of languages that are many hundreds of years old, including 16th and 17th century editions of famous authors such as Desiderius Erasmus, Horace, Julius Caesar, Machiavelli, Ovid, and Plutarch." Other highlights in Special Collections include an original edition of James Joyce's *Ulysses* (of which only 2,000 were printed), as well as a collection of 50 illuminated manuscripts from collector Dr. Otto Ege, an expert on medieval handwriting and illumination, who created teaching sets out of his manuscripts. In all, Special Collections claims more than 1,500 linear meters in published collections, including "quite a bit in terms of printing and printing presses."

A Common Mandate

Together, University Archives and Special Collections make for a formidable, unified collection, drawing between 1,500 and 2,000 researchers each year. "We've brought together both units in a holistic way," says Hutchinson. "We have a single reference desk now, for example." They also share a common mandate, focusing on the "acquisition, preservation, and accessibility of permanently valuable records of the University of Saskatchewan; and of books, journals, manuscripts, archival collections and printed ephemera of a rare, valuable or regional nature," as per the collection's website. Collection strengths are many, with a strong focus on western Canada and the Canadian Prairies ("Arthur Morton focused on that"), as well as a comprehensive LGBT collection that ranks in the "top three or four of its kind in the country." The Neil Richards Collection of Sexual and Gender Diversity contains rare and fragile titles, including LGBT periodicals, books by Canadian authors and publishers, queer mystery and detective fiction, and titles which predate the Stonewall Riots of 1969 and the beginning of the Gay Liberation Movement.

Other assorted strengths of the collection include an entire set of Audubon prints, a collection of early bibles even predating the King James Version (a 1541 English Bible printed by Edwarde Whitchurch), women's weekly magazines from the 1930s, a formidable set of Dickens materials, limited edition items from the Golden Cockerel Press (1920s to 1950s), and a host of materials from Saskatchewan publishers.

Moving on Up

"We've expanded over the years," says Hutchinson, "and now we have very active plans to move out of the [third] floor and onto the fifth floor, in its entirety." At present, UASC employs seven full-time equivalent employees: two archivists, one librarian, and four support staff. Hutchinson reports the move to the fifth floor will effectively double the overall footprint for University Archives & Special Collections, which will include space for compact shelving, an added classroom, and added storage. Now in the fundraising stages ("Until funding is lined up, nothing can be done"), the expansion would improve staff space and public service space alike, refurbishing the reading room and storage areas. "There is a committee actively working on [funding]," says Hutchinson, citing the possibility of a move within the next five or ten years.

Off-Site Locations

In addition to the space in Murray Library, University Archives & Special Collections also maintains two off-site locations: the first in the basement of a nearby chapel (holding materials that don't demand active reference), the second being the John G.

Diefenbaker Archives. Located on campus, the Diefenbaker Archives gathers the papers and books of John Diefenbaker, the 13th Prime Minister of Canada (1957-1963). It is one of only two collections of Prime Minister papers that aren't at Library and Archives Canada (the country's national archives). "Part of the [relocation] plan is to bring that all together in one place, on the fifth floor."

Acquisitions and Development

Supporting Teaching and Research

Hutchinson reports that while there is no formal collections policy for University Archives & Special Collections (outside of a formal mandate to acquire records of the university community), there is a general rule of thumb: "We look at what fits into the current collection." Much of this is concentrated on western Canada, and as always the collection looks to support research and teaching at the university. On a whole, acquisition duties are fairly informal within the unit, often dependent upon the extent of the proposed collection, although some acquisitions do require approval of library senior management.

In terms of funding, Hutchinson says there is revenue from some endowments, as well as other donations, available on the book acquisitions side, although such funds are not readily available for more general operations purposes. "The ones that do exist are used as a reliable resource," he says, citing funds for gay and lesbian materials in particular. While Hutchinson says there is one government grant lined up for a summer project, unfortunately the main source of regular external funding was cut by Library and Archives Canada. There are less reliable sources now than there were a few years ago.

Consistent Acquisitions

Still, acquisitions have remained constant, with Hutchinson reporting about 200 to 250 linear meters of archival acquisitions each year: about half university records and half external collections (donated archival materials). "For tax credits, we're appraising fifteen to twenty donations a year," he says. "Beyond that, we have a steady stream of ongoing acquisitions. For books, we have previously estimated 40 linear meters per year, but that may be on the low side: recent stats show approximately 3,000 equivalent volumes per year."

Although there are also space limitations to consider. With no university museum on campus, UASC does collect some artifacts, but their capabilities are limited. "We don't have the resources to accept everything that comes our way," says Hutchinson, "but there's not a lot of material offered to us that shouldn't be preserved, so if our institution isn't the beset fit, we'll try to find a good home for it."

Digitization

Digitizing Since the Dawn of the Web

"We've been digitizing for a long time," says Hutchinson, "pretty much since the Web started." He reports the first digitization projects at U of S to date back to the mid-1990s. "Then about ten years ago, we got into things in a more major way." This includes high resolution masters for all materials, as well as two tiers for most projects: a full database for the project, supplemented by thematic essays written by students and others. "We don't tend to be digitizing whole collections. We tend to focus on particular series and highlights. Lots of our digitization is done on demand from search requests.

"It's pretty much all theme-based," says Hutchinson of the materials they seek to digitize. "There's a site on northern Saskatchewan and northern Canada. There are sites that showcase different printing presses, for example." Collected on the UASC website (library.usask.ca/archives), these digital projects are sorted into ten main categories, each one full open access: *The Fine Arts and Photography*; *Gender and Sexuality*; *History and Politics*; *Literature*; *Native Studies*; *Northern Studies*; *Saskatchewan and Prairie Studies*; *Science and the Environment*; *Society and Culture*; and *University History*.

Much of this digitization work is grant-funded and for the most part has been handled in-house. "We've tended to hire internally," explains Hutchinson, citing the resources available to them to digitize right at the library: an automatic book scanner, an oversized scanner for map-sized items, and an automated slide scanner, among others. The slide scanner still gets frequent use, as University Archives & Special Collections has an extensive slide collection. "We're digitizing [slides] on a priority basis. With the Courtney Milne collection, for example, he shot hundreds of thousands of slides. So we're working through the material Milne identified as 'pick of the litter.' Forty-five thousand slides and counting." Another impressive slide digitization project documents the Peter MacKinnon Building, the U of S campus's oldest building and a National Historic Site of Canada. "They had a really extensive photo shoot of nearly every inch of the building," says Hutchinson, "and at the time, slides were the way to go."

Saskatchewan History Online (SHO)

The largest project in scope the University Library has undertaken is the Saskatchewan History Online (SHO), a three-year initiative that will come to a head before year's end. Funded by the Saskatchewan Ministry of Education and in collaboration with the Saskatchewan Digital Alliance (a committee of the Multitype Library Board), the project looks to "increase the availability of free online access to Saskatchewan's cultural and historical record," as per the project's website (saskhistoryonline.ca). The SHO technological infrastructure is built for exploration, use, and storage of digitized cultural heritage materials, “and [U of S Library] served as the technical hub,” says Hutchinson.

Digital Preservation

“We’re more actively getting into digital preservation,” reports Hutchinson. “We’re trying to create a framework for digital records.” At present, UASC is in the process of moving over to Archivematica, an open-source digital preservation system, which packages the digital material and metadata. “In the next few months we’ll be able to use it in production. And we’ve also contracted the vendor to integrate with the software we use for Islandora, so we can preserve the digital originals.”

Outreach and Exhibits

A New Department, a New Website

As part of the merger establishing the new department, University Archives & Special Collections launched a new website. The website, whose launch coincided with a transfer to a new content management system, features a diligently active newsfeed. “We highlight ways that our collections have been used.” Hutchinson also reports they are working on a project to get finding aids online.

Promoting the Collection

“Quite a range of classes have used the Archives and Special Collections,” says Hutchinson, citing not just the usual departments of History and Political Science but also those departments off the beaten path such as Sociology, Kinesiology (the history of sport), Art and Art History (printmaking), and an interdisciplinary Cultural Heritage Mapping class. “We’ve been quite active with outreach over the years, often in collaboration with the Saskatchewan Council for Archives and Archivists.” Of late, Hutchinson cites a recently released series of short films, available on YouTube, or else the video series “The Truth Is in There,” showcasing the University Archives and other repositories across the province. University Archives & Special Collections has also done a lot with local publications, including a regular column in *On Campus News* (the university's official employee newspaper published 18 times per year) and a regular feature in the *Green & White* alumni newsletter. Hutchinson reports that the library's images are also often used by University Advancement. A highlight of the year is Archives Week, celebrated every February and featuring events such as "Spotlight on the Past: Celebrity Readings from Archives in Saskatchewan."

Exhibits and Exhibit Space

The main exhibit space available to UASC is located on the first floor of Murray Library. Connecting the old building with the new building, Link Gallery was refurbished three years ago and holds exhibits for approximately three or four months at a time. "We use it generally to showcase our collections," says Hutchinson, "but we also invite curators from other parts of the library to participate as well. [Link Gallery] has a good range of cases, the ability to put posters up, slideshow capabilities, etcetera." Hutchinson and his colleagues also have at their disposal a few small display cases in the reading room ("In the last few months, we've started tying that to another display case on the ground floor, next to a Starbucks. Increased foot traffic!") as well as a display case in the main administration building, the Peter MacKinnon Building. The display case has room for an upright display model and is used primarily for reproductions of card stock. "It's a good way to display our collections outside the library." University Archives & Special Collections shares the space with the art gallery and the museum of antiquities (again, putting on about three or four exhibitions a year). "Occasionally, do we get special exhibits requests for alumni events as well."

Exhibits tend to be more curated, Hutchinson says. "It's not just about the collection itself, but about bringing a few different collections together to showcase the range of what we have." This includes both newer collections and time-tested collection strengths alike. The current exhibit, for example, is on printmaking, which includes the works of several local artists who created original prints. Or else there was the recent exhibit, *Judge a Book by Its Cover: The Physicality of the Book*, which explored the physical significance of the book. Last fall, *QueerUS: Language, Space, and the University of Saskatchewan* highlighted the rich history and presence of queer culture in Saskatoon. In addition, every few years a university author's exhibit showcases books by U of S faculty.

Lending and Conservation

University Archives & Special Collections lends out materials occasionally, as long as the location has proper security and facilities (such as locked display cases). "[Lending] hasn't come up a huge amount," says Hutchinson. "It's tended to be galleries when it has." Security and theft on a whole, either at the library or away from it, has never been a cause for concern. "But it is certainly something we pay attention to," adds Hutchinson.

Concerning conservation of the materials, Hutchinson reports that without a conservation lab, the focus is placed on collection management and proper handling: "We try to keep things as controlled as we can [when handling the materials]." He adds that the proposed move to the fifth floor would address some issues with controlling humidity and temperature. "We rely on the relatively dry climate of Saskatchewan."

SPECIAL COLLECTIONS & ARCHIVES, HAMILTON COLLEGE

We spoke with Christian Goodwillie, Director and Curator of Special Collections & Archives at Hamilton College. Initially hired as Curator of Special Collections in 2009, Goodwillie has also served as Director of Special Collections & Archives since the department's inception in 2011.

General Description

The Third Oldest College in New York State

Hamilton College was originally founded in 1793 as the Hamilton-Oneida Academy by Presbyterian minister and missionary Samuel Kirkland. It was named for statesman Alexander Hamilton, who consented to be a trustee, and received its college charter from the Regents of the State University of New York in 1812. Located in the Village of Clinton in Central New York, Hamilton stands as the third oldest college in New York State, behind only Columbia University and Union College. With roots that date back over two centuries, the institution's collections extend wide and far—including Samuel Kirkland's own books and papers.

By the mid-20th century, a dedicated space known as the "Treasure Room" had been established in the James Library (now the Christian A. Johnson Building) for rare books and archival materials, with Kirkland's papers included. This coincided with an increased focus on rare book collecting. "Obviously, an incredible amount of material had accumulated over the years," says Goodwillie. These materials were subsequently moved to the Daniel Burke Library upon the library's completion in 1972, where the materials have stayed ever since—although it was not until 2011 that Special Collections & Archives came together as an official unit.

The Creation of Special Collections & Archives

Goodwillie was hired as Curator of Special Collections two years prior, in 2009. At that time, Special Collections and Archives remained separate, and when the position was created, Goodwillie's main responsibilities as newly-appointed Curator were threefold: 1) to integrate the use of Special Collections into the academic program, working with faculty and students, 2) to continue to collect and build the collections, working with book dealers and scholars, and 3) to deal with the large backlog of materials. "A lot of it had been cataloged already," says Goodwillie of the backlog, "but there were easily eighty boxes of materials that were still waiting [to be cataloged], by no fault of the previous librarian. They could only do so much without a position dedicated solely to sorting through the materials and deciding what to catalog and what to dispose of."

In 2011, then, the department of Special Collections & Archives was created and settled into its newly-constructed space on the third floor of Burke Library, a space that includes ample storage area, office space, a departmental coordinator's office, as well as a reading and exhibit room. The Archives are located three floors below in the library's basement, along with three other dedicated storage units. The department remains relatively small: in addition to Goodwillie, Special Collections & Archives employs a college archivist (0.6 FTE), a digital imagery specialist (1 FTE), a departmental coordinator (1 FTE), and a jazz archivist (0.5 FTE). "But we work very closely with the Library Information Systems people too," adds Goodwillie, "as well as the Technical Services department," the latter of which handles cataloging and metadata for the digital collections. "My role as Curator is to supply them with a lot of the information they need beyond simple bibliographic data."

With a department this small, part of Goodwillie's job is to determine "which collections [we] want to catalog. There were massive collections of unprocessed material on site," he says, "so it was a tremendous workload for all departments involved." Sometimes this involves finding better homes for prospective materials elsewhere (through book dealers, for example), or simply prioritizing what gets cataloged ("almanacs are a priority"). Likewise, Goodwillie recognizes the demands on the college archivist cannot be met fully by a 0.6 FTE position. "This makes it hard for the Archives to accomplish the three big goals of college archives," which Goodwillie lists as 1) patron requests, 2) backlog and digitization stream, and 3) collecting. While Goodwillie reports that the backlog has nearly been whittled down to nothing, at least on the Special Collections side, a huge influx of recent donations to the Archives has lengthened the process, adding more than 60 boxes of papers to the queue.

The Beinecke Lesser Antilles Collection

Among the institution's many collecting strengths, Special Collections & Archives at Hamilton showcases three premiere collections, each set claiming distinctive and unique holdings rarely found elsewhere. Perhaps the most impressive of these three collections is the Beinecke Lesser Antilles Collection. Gifted to the Hamilton College Library by the Beinecke family (the driving force behind such philanthropic endeavors as the Beinecke Rare Book and Manuscript Library at Yale University), it stands as the preeminent collection of materials on the Lesser Antilles. "It's probably the best collection of Caribbean [materials] in one place outside the Caribbean," says Goodwillie. The collection features manuscript materials from the early 17th century up to the early 20th century (with the bulk of these materials dating to the 18th century), as well as a few thousand imprints (either printed in the Caribbean or relating to the Caribbean) dating to the 16th century. "The materials and manuscripts are in a variety of languages," says Goodwillie. "There's a lot of French and Spanish, some English, a smattering of Dutch and Swedish." An accompanying collection of maps and prints (oil paintings and watercolors) are also featured prominently in the Beinecke Collection, some of which are held in the Ruth and Elmer Wellin Museum of Art on campus.

"It's a collection that has worldwide demand," says Goodwillie. "So many scholars trying to use it are from Europe or the Caribbean." As such, for the sake of preservation and increased accessibility, a great deal of effort has been made to digitize the Beinecke Collection, based largely on requests from researchers. Goodwillie reports they are "nearly finished digitizing all the manuscripts," all of which are made available for free. Tackled entirely in-house, Goodwillie estimates the digitization of the Beinecke Collection should take approximately three years from start to finish.

The Ezra Pound Collection

Also of great renown is the Ezra Pound Collection, which features over 2,500 manuscripts, correspondences, books owned and used by Ezra Pound, foreign translations, and photographs—as well as first editions of all but two of the poet's works. Pound attended Hamilton College from 1903-1905, as did his son Omar five decades later, who befriended the College Librarian, Walter Pilkington. Upon Omar's death in 2010, his widow Elizabeth donated a substantial number of manuscripts to the college. "[The collection] is very strong in primary and secondary resources," explains Goodwillie. "The manuscript collection is mostly correspondences between Pound and his wife [Dorothy Shakespear], but also between Omar and his parents, as well as a lot of other correspondence of his."

Goodwillie explains that the materials in the Pound Collection fall into three general levels of accessibility. The first tier, which includes the majority of material, is fully and freely available to the public. The next tier includes materials that are available only with written permission from the Pound family. Beyond that, however, are the restricted correspondences, the parameters of which remain unclear to Goodwillie himself. "Pound is an interesting character to Hamilton College," he explains. "It's kind of a mixed blessing. On the one hand, he was a literary genius and a mentor. But his politics were fairly controversial," he says, referring to Pound's fascist sympathies during World War II. "But I give the family a tremendous amount of credit [for making much of this material available]."

The Communal Societies Collection

The last of these three main collections is the Communal Societies Collection, which gathers approximately 2,500 items on communal societies, with a particular emphasis on the Shakers (including an exhaustive digitization project of *The Shaker Manifesto*—or simply *The Manifesto* as it was later known—the official journal of the Shakers). The collection gathers manuscripts, printed works, visual materials, audio and video materials, ephemera, and a limited number of artifacts. Former Hamilton College Librarian Ralph Stenstrom, who served from 1975 to 2000, focused collection efforts on materials relating to the "burned-over" district (a mission continued by his successor, Randy Ericson). The burned-over district was a hotbed of religious revivalism in Western and Central New York in the 19th century, so named due to the area's heavy evangelizing that left few populations unconverted, with no "fuel" left to "burn." In addition to the Shakers, who established their first communal farm in the area, the burned-over district was home to a host of religious sects, including the Mormons and the Oneida Society, the latter of which believed in Christian Perfectionism, living free from sin. "The Oneida Community practiced Complex Marriage," explains Goodwillie, a form of free love in which members are permitted to have sex with any other consenting member, "and they also had a form of birth control, practicing male continence. They are widely acknowledged as engaging the world's first eugenics program, too."

The Communal Societies Collection features one of the best gatherings of printed primary and secondary materials relating to American intentional communities, both religious and secular, dating as far back as the 17th century and leading to the present. Collected here is an impressive manuscript archive of one former member of Rajneeshpuram, the intentional community based out of Oregon in the 1980s. The Florida-based Koreshan Unity is also well represented in the collection, thanks to a recent acquisition that makes Hamilton College one of the only libraries with such materials—just as it boasts the largest manuscript collection of the Israelite House of David, one of only three or four places in the world to collect these materials. "We're trying to create a niche for ourselves on the internet," says Goodwillie, powered by huge manuscript collections from the Shakers and the Harmony Society. Other communities that are well represented in the collection include the Amana Colonies, the Society of Separatists at Zoar, and the Ruskin Commongood Society.

The Communal Societies Collection benefits from a generous endowment left by Hamilton alumnus Richard W. Couper and his wife Patricia. "They gave a huge endowment that allowed Randy [Ericson] to build the collection to this level," relates Goodwillie, "to one of the best—if not the best—in the country." Upon the Mr. Couper's death in 2006, Ericson also established the Richard W. Couper Press, which to date has published more than 20 monographs, and a quarterly journal of scholarship promoting the collection, the *American Communal Societies Quarterly (ACSQ)*, currently in its eighth volume.

Acquisitions and Development

Healthy Acquisitions

"In general, acquisitions are my responsibility," says Goodwillie. "Of course I'm always open to faculty saying, 'I'm going to be teaching X course, and I'd love to have this book to use.'" Goodwillie says that potentially substantial acquisitions outside the three main collections require discussion with the library director, although he also relates a healthy number of available acquisition streams. There is a large operating line for conservation in general, and of course the very substantial endowment provided by the Coupers. In fact, for the most part Goodwillie relates that acquisitions have increased over the last few years. "Hamilton has been very fortunate to continue aggressively building our collections, even during the recession."

In terms of donated collections, Goodwillie reports that the college receives such offers a couple times a year. “We haven’t had to turn anything down so far,” he says. “This would only happen if [the proposed donation] wasn’t appropriate or didn’t fit with our collection.” The other responsibility behind taking on such acquisitions, whether they are donated or otherwise, lies in the ability to make use of the materials. “It’s the bane of any archive or rare book collection, and of any scholar or researcher, not to have the resources to make the materials available and accessible. That’s why we put so much effort here to get rid of that backlog.”

Digitization

A Wealth of Resources, and Still More to Come

The digitization efforts of Special Collections & Archives started years before Goodwillie’s arrival at Hamilton. Such projects included Samuel Kirkland’s original papers, a large collection of Civil War letters, and the entire Shaker periodical run, dating from 1871 to 1899 and totaling 16 volumes, 349 issues, and 8,136 pages. “Then once I got here, we continued with the Communal Societies [materials].” These materials, along with all the digitized works, are all fully accessible via the digital collection’s website (http://elib.hamilton.edu), and while the digitization process is ongoing, a wealth of resources are already readily available. The Communal Societies Collection, for example, currently features nine dropdown menus of collected digital sets, from the Amana Society to Snow Hill Cloister.

As with his acquisition duties, Goodwillie is responsible for determining what materials gets digitized, often consulting with the college archivist and entertaining external requests as they arise (which is how the digitization of the Beinecke Collection, now nearing completion, came about). As was the case with the Beinecke Collection, most digitization work for Special Collections & Archives is handled in-house. “We’re fortunate enough to have a full-time person with the expertise to handle digitizing, so when we weigh the pros and cons of outsourcing digitization, it's more financially efficient to do it in-house." An added benefit: diminished risk of damage to materials due to excess travel and handling.

The next large-scale digitization project on the horizon for Special Collections & Archives is the collected newspapers of Father Divine, the spiritual leader of the International Peace Mission movement. The son of slaves, Father Divine was an egalitarian, building up a sizable evangelical following in the 1930s and eventually settling outside of Philadelphia. "We're going to be getting one copy of each printed item," says Goodwillie, all of which will be put online.

The Beloved Witness Project

Beyond that, Special Collections & Archives recently acquired the papers of the late poet Agha Shahid Ali, a former Hamilton College faculty member and native of Kashmir, India who passed away in 2001. "His poetry has become important to people in both India and Pakistan," says Goodwillie, "as well as becoming very important internationally." The materials, including manuscripts and correspondences, were acquired through Pat O'Neill, Professor of English at Hamilton College and friend of the late poet and his family. O'Neill is working closely with the Digital Humanities Initiative (DHi) at Hamilton on "The Beloved Witness," a project to digitize and archive the poet's documents, letters, and manuscripts. Says Goodwillie: "We're hosting a symposium here in September focusing on his poetry, so we hope to have at least the first part of the collection digitized by then."

Outreach and Exhibitions

Word of Mouth

"We don't pay any attention to social media," admits Goodwillie. "I get a hundred emails a day without that!" Special Collections & Archives thrives, instead, on word of mouth within the small and active community. "We get so much word of mouth from the scholars and researchers that we always have a lot to do." Goodwillie also has modest in-house public relations capabilities at his disposal, a unit that will post news and notifications on the library's homepage. "Occasionally things will rise to the level of the College's communications department," he says, "in which case updates can be posted to the [Hamilton College] website. This past year, the communications department featured Special Collections & Archives prominently in a number of news stories and college publications, which has been very helpful in raising awareness of what we're doing." In terms of media beyond that, however, Goodwillie relates that there is not a lot of exposure outside of academic journals, such as with the *American Communal Societies Quarterly*.

Exhibits

Special Collections & Archives has exhibition space on all three floors of Burke Library, which it uses to mount at least two, and sometimes three, exhibitions per year. This spread-out placement is ideal for drawing in guests, inviting patrons to "start in the main lobby and ultimately move up to [Special Collections & Archives on] the third floor." In addition to these in-house exhibits and displays, Goodwillie is open to lending materials from the collection to outside institutions from time to time, "especially if it's someone I know." Goodwillie is a strong advocate of making materials "as available as possible to researchers and scholars," adding that it is "inexcusable to make people jump through hoops to get access to information."

Advice to Peers

Treasures in the Stacks

Goodwillie has some parting advice for his peers, having observed a few things through his experiences dealing with public and academic libraries. "I've seen a lot of different institutions," he says, "and I'm shocked at how casually materials are disposed of sometimes." As he sees it, there is a missed opportunity here, citing an imaginary dividing line that is often put up between special collections and the general stacks in libraries, and Goodwillie recognizes a more efficient way to withdraw books from the stacks: "Use them as an asset, as the valuable resources they are. We sell these withdrawn books through an Amazon account we maintain internally."

On top of this, Goodwillie finds great value in looking through the general stacks for hidden gems. "This library is small enough to do that, about 600,000 volumes, and we've been able to uncover a lot of books from the original collection, just sitting there on the stacks. As all our institutions age," Goodwillie continues, "it is well worth the effort to look inside. There are treasures that have been hiding in plain sight." Goodwillie relates a story of a librarian at Washington University in St. Louis, Missouri, who realized that a book in the rare book collection had once belonged to Thomas Jefferson. "Following up on that clue, they discovered nearly seventy of Jefferson's books in their collection of which they were previously unaware. It turned out to be something like the third largest collection!" Closer to home, Goodwillie found a first edition of Alexander Hamilton's papers in the stacks at Burke Library, a copy which was later discovered to belong to Hamilton's widow. "It's by no means the fault of anyone before me [at Hamilton]. There's just a lot out there. But it's worth it to see what's hiding in the stacks. It's a great opportunity for most large collections."

SPECIAL COLLECTIONS AND ARCHIVES (SCOLAR), CARDIFF UNIVERSITY

We spoke with Peter Keelan, Head of Cardiff University's Special Collections and Archives (SCOLAR). Keelan has held this position since SCOLAR's inception in 2005.

General Description

Over 120 Years in the Making

Founded in 1883, Cardiff University (initially named the University College of South Wales and Monmouthshire) now stands as the largest research university in Wales, and in less than 150 years it has established itself also as one of Britain's leading teaching and research universities. While rare book collecting at Cardiff has been a practice nearly since the university's foundation, it was not until 2005 that it all came together in one place: with the merging of Cardiff University and the University of Wales College of Medicine the year before, the rich history of rare book collecting at Cardiff had become apparent to newly-named Cardiff Librarian Steve Pritchard (previously with the College of Medicine), and so Special Collections and Archives (SCOLAR) was swiftly established, with Keelan appointed as SCOLAR's first (and, since then, only) Head.

Keelan estimates the collections that came together under SCOLAR had been scattered across a dozen different libraries. "We've integrated most of them here into SCOLAR," he says of the collections, which were previously managed by individual subject librarians. Now housed on the ground floor of the Arts and Social Studies Library (the university's main library)—where it has been since its foundation—SCOLAR boasts up to 100,000 volumes of pre-20th century materials, as well as an additional 70,000 volumes of 21st century materials, plus a wide range of 18th to 20th century archives. The university's first collection was acquired in 1886, "and we've been adding to that collection ever since."

The Salisbury Collection

That founding collection was the Salisbury Library collection, acquired by the university in 1886 from Flintshire businessman and bibliophile Enoch Robert Gibbon Salisbury. Salisbury's personal library included rare books and albums of maps and prints of Welsh and Border Counties focus, with some of these materials dating as far back as the 16th century. Since that initial acquisition, the already strong collection has continued to thrive, growing into one of the major collections of its kind about Wales and wider Celtic studies, a collection now of international significance.

The Cardiff Rare Books Collection

More recent strengths have risen from the university's 2010 acquisition of the Cardiff Central Library's rare book collection. Acquired from the Cardiff City Council for £1.2 million, the acquisition was an instant boon to SCOLAR. "As a public library, [Cardiff Central Library] was catering more for popular reading not using rare books as much," explains Keelan, and so the collection was acquired by SCOLAR, where it retained its original name, the Cardiff Rare Books Collection. Bringing together over 14,000 books from the 15th century onward, the collection covers British and European studies, but has highlights in three distinctive collection areas of both national and international import. The first is an extraordinary set of British private press books, the most famous of which is William Morris's Kelmscott Press. "It's one of the two largest collections in Britain, and the world," says Keelan. Another strength is a world-class collection of English Restoration dramas from the late 17th century, "including almost everything by [John] Dryden," as well as various Shakespearean second and third editions. The third highlight is the incunabula collection, which gathers about 180 works published between 1470 and 1500, including some of the earliest printed books in Europe from the Gutenberg era, the start of modern printing in Europe. "There are only three incunabula collections in Wales," says Keelan, "and this is one of them."

Human and Medical Genetics Historical Library

Outside of the humanities rare books collection, SCOLAR also lays claim to very strong collections in medicine, one of the most notable of which is the Human and Medical Genetics Historical Library. Established in 2003 by Professor Peter Harper, this special collection chronicles the development of human genetics, and with roughly 4,000 volumes of 20th century books and monographs, the collection stands as the only one of its kind, and yet another collection of international significance.

Other Collections of National Significance

Keelan is keen to point out a handful of other collections at SCOLAR that are particularly noteworthy from a Welsh and U.K. perspective. One such strength is a collection of 19th century children's literature, featuring English and Welsh children's books, journals, and comics, as well as a wide variety of rare illustrated books, booklets, and almanacs. The personal archive and book collection of World War I poet Edward Thomas is another collection of great importance, brining together the poet's papers, poems, and correspondences, the largest collection of its kind in the world. Keelan also mentions an historical travel writing collection of about 3,000 volumes, including topography and travel collections dating back to the 17th, 18th, and 19th centuries, with Baedecker guides, and various 20th century tourist writings. "It's a developing research field," Keelan says of the travel writing collection. "We find it's being dipped into a lot at the moment."

Acquisitions and Development

Diversifying the Funding Base

SCOLAR does not benefit from the luxury of an acquisitions budget, and so Keelan estimates that 90 percent of the library's acquisitions come from donations (with the £1.2 million acquisition of the rare books collection being the big exception).

Grants and other assorted funding sources do materialize on an ad hoc basis (SCOLAR liaises close with the head of Alumni and Development, who is responsible for fundraising), and Keelan stresses that SCOLAR is active in seeking out funding and regularly brings in funds for "cataloging, conservation, and digitization." But when it comes to acquisitions, Keelan relates that funding is not as easy to come by: "Because of the recession here, our usual sources of funding are drying up. So we're having to diversify the funding base." As such, SCOLAR must look to a much wider range of funding bodies. "But we're all facing the same situation," says Keelan of the recession. Considering the library funding and donors culture in the United Kingdom, Keelan reports that "[the U.K.] is decades behind the United States. And our alumni staff is aware of this. But most universities in the U.K. just haven't had that approach to philanthropic culture, not until the last five or ten years."

Acquisitions Duties

All of SCOLAR's acquisition decisions are made by Keelan, who liaises with relevant academic staff for specific subjects or collections. For large donations he has at his disposal an advisory committee, the SCOLAR Strategy Group, which meets four times each year. "I bring information to them on the collections we're offered," he says of the committee. These offers will come from retiring academics, friends of the university, members of the public, etc. The group consists of about a dozen internal members of the university, such as Professor Bill Bell who chairs the group, the head of Alumni and Development, several subject librarians, as well as two external special consultants: Baroness Kay Andrews from the House of Lords, and Dr. Aled Jones, Chief Executive and Librarian of the National Library of Wales.

A Steady Stream of Donations

"At Cardiff, we've had a non-stop stream of offers of donations and collections," says Keelan. "The situation is looking healthy for us. We regularly get offered materials every year." Keelan goes on to say that because of the recession, the public library sector is being hit exceptionally hard with funding cuts, and as such the public libraries are withdrawing from accepting donations, thus leaving the window open for the university libraries.

With an estimated 90 percent of SCOLAR's acquisitions comprised of donations, the offers that come to Keelan understandably run the gamut of size and breadth. Some have been small, others have been larger. Recent donation offers include a collection of the papers of British philosopher R.G. Collingwood and his family, as well as a series of papers from Victorian era art critic John Ruskin. SCOLAR also acquired a collection of historical manuscripts and scores from the BBC Library when it was closing down. Also completely donated is the Human and Medical Genetics Historical Library.

Another prime example of donated collections at SCOLAR is the Sir Iain Chalmers archive. Chalmers was one of the founders of the Cochrane Collaboration, an independent non-profit organization formed to organize medical research information in a systematic way and a culmination of the work of Archie Cochrane. Cochrane, a staff professor at Cardiff in the 1960s, pioneered the study and practice of evidence-based healthcare. His work advocated for the use of randomized control trials to make medicine more effective and efficient. The archive collects the personal papers of Chalmers, himself a leading proponent of evidence-based healthcare, plus many of his colleagues in this field, documenting the British researcher's attendance at conferences and symposiums, service on committees, forums, working parties, as well as teaching, publication, and external duties in higher education.

Says Keelan of what SCOLAR looks for in donations: "We have a range of subject areas in which we're still developing, such as in humanities and social sciences, as well as history of medicine, and modern journalism papers and popular presses such as the Daily Mirror." Keelan emphasizes that donations, as with all acquisitions, are of particular interest to SCOLAR when especially aligned with the university's research fields or teaching modules.

Digitization

Teaching and Research Priorities

SCOLAR's first digitization project dates back to 2002, when Keelan initiated, with academic staff from the Welsh department, the digitization of the library's 19th century collection. Funded by £10,000 of internal university money, the goal of that project was to make materials more accessible for both teaching and research—a goal which has extended to the library's ongoing digitization efforts today. "We've looked at what other people have done elsewhere," Keelan says of the efforts of his peers, "and what they've often done is cherry pick [from their collections], so it all looks very nice. But there seemed no academic rationale to it. What we focus on is teaching and research priorities."

In 2009, SCOLAR digitized about half a dozen collections more, including collections in architecture, history of medicine, history of pharmacy, and institutional university history. These collections were launched in SCOLAR's DigitalSearch repository, which is linked on the library's catalog and website (http://digitalsearch.cf.ac.uk). The digitization projects at SCOLAR are all full open access, and in time the library will be transferring the initial 19th century collection to this platform as well. SCOLAR was also the first library in Wales to adopt Turning the Pages™, the digital software developed by the British Library. "It was years ahead of the iPad," says Keelan. "We got a grant to install two of those in the university library, and to digitize about a dozen books for that."

Looking forward, SCOLAR has already surveyed all of the academic schools across campus, culling responses from a dozen academics with preferences on what they'd like to see digitized. Keelan anticipates the same will happen next year as SCOLAR looks to build its digital collections even further. "It follows academic priorities for teaching in the university," he stresses. All digitization work for SCOLAR is completed in-house. "We do the metadata, we do the cataloging, we do the scanning and file preservation, plus the digital ingest into DigitalSearch. There are staff resources devoted to this." Keelan explains the library has built up a team with a wide range of capabilities. "We're the only university library in Wales which has that expertise in-house. The National Library of Wales is really the only other one, and we have cooperated with them on joint digitization projects also, most recently on the World War I archives."

Outreach and Publicity

An Active Website

Keelan describes SCOLAR's website (http://www.cardiff.ac.uk/insrv/libraries/scolar) as "a key shop window into not just our collections, but the work we do as well." He considers keeping the website current and filled "almost our number one priority," and great strides have been taken to make sure that promise is fulfilled. For example, within the past 12 months SCOLAR has added collection-level descriptions for just about every collection. "It's been talked about in library reports for years, because it's been lacking in the U.K.," Keelan says of collection descriptions. SCOLAR received a modest grant of £15,000 from the National Assembly for Wales, and with that they have been able to add descriptions to nearly 150 collections, from classical, to early modern, to the 20th century. "The aim is to keep it simple [for patrons]," and SCOLAR appears unique among universities in the U.K. as it categorizes its collections not only alphabetically by title, but chronologically. "We're the only ones to break it up by chronological era," says Keelan. "No other university in the U.K. apparently does that."

Public Relations and Social Media

SCOLAR shares a communications team with the I.T. department, a team which handles all publicity for the library and consists of three or four staff members. Says Keelan: "They're very helpful. [We go to them] anytime we want something pushed out, within the university or else outside to the newspapers." This communications team frequently drafts up press releases and disseminates them among their media contacts. In addition, SCOLAR also maintains an active blog (http://scolarcardiff.wordpress.com), which receives about 20,000 views per year. Updated every few weeks, the blog is a vehicle to post about a new volume that's been cataloged, or to profile treasures in the collection (such as a recently discovered long-last rare book from the library of Sir Isaac Newton).

Keelan sees a great need to be active with the library's outreach, and so SCOLAR puts a concerted effort into promotion and marketing. "Because we're a specialist niche market, we've got to be selling our wares all the time. To new staff, new students, new university vice chancellors." As such, "digitization, outreach, and publicity are all in the same bag."

Exhibits

A Robust Exhibition Schedule

Available to SCOLAR are seven museum-grade exhibition cabinets, located in the SCOLAR entrance foyer, acting as a shop window. Also in this space, which measures roughly 50 meters by 35 meters, is the Turning the Pages™ exhibit. SCOLAR utilizes all these platforms to showcase three new exhibitions each year. "We've done about 20 exhibitions since 2007," Keelan says, adding that the exhibition schedule is set at least a year in advance. In conjunction with each exhibit, SCOLAR also takes digital snapshots of the items on display and puts the images on their website. "This way, across the world, people can get a flavor of what collections we have."

Upcoming Exhibits

SCOLAR's current display was coordinated by the PhD program in the English department, an exhibit on modern medievalists that highlights the 19th and 20th century obsession with reproducing medieval-type works in private presses. Another exhibit is slated for summer, in which one of the lecturers in the English department will present her work chronicling the history of women in trousers, tackling question as to why women began wearing trousers and shining light on society's initial response. "All the illustrations needed for the exhibit were found in SCOLAR," says Keelan. Even farther down the line, an exhibition on World War II is planned for the end of the year, to coincide with a conference by the humanities schools.

Preservation

Archive Accreditation

"Raising money for preservation is difficult," reports Keelan. "So the big thing in the U.K. at the moment is a new accreditation scheme called the Archive Service Accreditation." As per the organization's website, this new standard "defines good practice and identifies agreed standards, thereby encouraging and supporting development." Should an archive meet the minimum national standard, it will receive a government stamp of approval as a badge of recognition, which Keelan is confident will lead to increased funding. SCOLAR is applying for this designation within the next two years.

Security

Not an Issue

"Security is not a big issue for us," Keelan says, and while SCOLAR has never had any serious problems with theft, the library has nonetheless been diligent in improving security over the years. Additional close-circuit television monitors have been installed, as well as additional alarms on the rare book stacks. Supervision in the reading room has improved, and locks have been upgraded. "We're conscious of all the usual [concerns], and we address issues as they come up."

ARCHIVES & SPECIAL COLLECTIONS, AMHERST COLLEGE

We spoke with Mike Kelly, Head of Archives & Special Collections at Amherst College, who recently celebrated his five-year anniversary in this position.

General Description

Introduction and Strengths

Archives & Special Collections at Amherst College is known for a great many collecting strengths, as could be expected from one of the nation's premier liberal arts colleges. Located in idyllic Western Massachusetts on a 1,000-acre campus, the college stands as the third oldest institution of higher education in the state, with strong alumni ties and a diverse history steeped in charity and service, all supported by extensive physical resources. As such, "[our] collection is an interesting amalgamation," explains Kelly, citing both obvious and well-known strengths alongside more esoteric yet exhaustive treasures.

Housed in Robert Frost Library—the college's main library—Archives & Special Collections understandably boasts a significant Robert Frost collection. Having taught at the college on and off for more than 40 years, the American poet is one of Amherst's best-known faculty, and Frost's history with the college is intertwined with the history of the college itself. Frost Library opened in 1965, just two years after the poet's death (though the poet was still alive in 1962 when Amherst first announced its new library was to be named for him), and the library still serves as the college's home for collections in the arts, humanities, and social sciences, as well as general interest science materials. Archives & Special Collections is located on A-level of the six-floor library.

"There were a lot of different collections that came together when Frost [Library] was built," says Kelly, "and while 1965 is when it all came together physically, 1979 is when it became *official*," when the college's Board of Trustees issued a mandate creating the official Amherst College Archives for the permanent preservation of records of academic programs and courses, official records of administrators and administrative offices, and those materials with permanent historical value.

The Archives also maintains a great Emily Dickinson collection, one of the largest in the country. Dickinson, like Frost, has deep-rooted ties to Amherst College: her grandfather, Samuel Fowler Dickinson, was one of the founders of the college while her father, Edward Dickinson, served as College Treasurer from 1835 to 1873. The Dickinson collection includes original poems, manuscripts, and letters from Dickinson to family and friends, along with images of the poet, physical artifacts, transcriptions, printers' copies and proofs, and all sorts of Dickinson-related materials.

Beyond Frost and Dickinson

"Those are the obvious ones," Kelly says in reference to the Frost and Dickinson collections. But Archives & Special Collections also keeps impressive and unique holdings in history of science collections, with some materials dating back to the early 19th century. One such example is the work of Edward Hitchcock. A former geology professor and eventual President of the college, Hitchcock made a name for himself studying and collecting dinosaur tracks. "We have the books he was using, as well as his papers," says Kelly, adding that Hitchcock was one of the first and few at the time to believe the fossilized footmarks to be the marks of gigantic birds. "We have tons of this material.

"And it's the same with ornithology," Kelly continues. "We've had faculty that were just really serious about birds." Indeed, prominent elements of the Archives are reflections of the varied interests and studies of past alumni, faculty, and Amherst scholars. A strong astronomy collection is very much the product of Amherst's own observatory—built in 1847, the building known as the Octagon still stands on campus, although it no longer serves as a functioning observatory. Religious texts are also well represented in the Archives, owing to Amherst's origins as an institution founded for the "education of indigent young men of piety and talents for the Christian ministry," (as related on the college's website). "We also have travel books," says Kelly, "of the Middle East, Syria. All those [missionaries] that went there in the thirties, they came back and donated all their materials." These missionary diaries include exclusive and exceptional source materials that are unlikely to be found elsewhere, such as eyewitness accounts of Armenian genocide.

In all, Archives & Special Collections holds between 80,000 and 90,000 rare books, which Kelly deems a "manageable collection," with nearly 300 discreet manuscripts totaling between 15,000 and 18,000 linear feet. This adds up to a vast and varied collection, not just limited to the works of its famous poets, but serving, as Kelly calls it, as a "snapshot of nineteenth century missionary culture with a dose of science."

Acquisitions and Development

A Renewed Mission Statement

The mission of Archives & Special Collections is to support the teaching and research of students and faculty, and during his time as Head of the Archives, Kelly has worked hard to establish and enforce this purpose. "This was my mission coming here," he says, "to change it from that precious, fine printing, old book whatever-they-want-to-give-us collection, to filling in the gaps for existing strengths and focusing on research and teaching." All acquisition duties fall squarely on Kelly's shoulders, an ideal situation as he sees it. "It's all me," he says with a laugh, although he has plenty of support when he needs it, including from his new director. "It really is [that] we're trying to shift a whole culture," Kelly says, noting that he and his director are fully on the same page with the shift. The goal is not just to serve the alumni, but to foster a culture of being serious academics while establishing the collection as one that supports students and faculty. Kelly recognizes this mission to be very much in step with the general mission of the college: "Lots of faculty-student attention, lots of emphasis on teaching. And we're trying to get more aligned with that." In this spirit, the Archives is a training collection, too, as Kelly identifies a need for Amherst students to learn how to work with rare books, particularly in a safe and familiar environment. The department itself is small, with plenty of student help: there are two full-time professionals on staff (including Kelly), three FTE non-professionals, and a handful of student workers. "Lately, we've also had a fairly good influx of interns from the library program at Simmons College, students looking for archives experience."

Donations and Gifts

Strong alumni ties and the donations they bring to the library are an asset to any special collection, envied by every special collections librarian. "Historically, we've had strong and steady gifts from alumni," says Kelly, and this is the case not just for Archives & Special Collections, but for the college as a whole: according to the college's website, more than 60 percent of Amherst's alumni make a gift to the college each year—among the highest alumni participation rates in the country. "[Donations to the Archives] include everything from students who knew Robert Frost back in the forties and fifties to this one strong collector who collects everything James Merrill (poet and Amherst alum) ever published, including signed press printings." One such donated gem in the Archives is a copy of the Shakespeare Second Folio: dating to 1632, the folio used to belong to one of Amherst's fraternities.

But with the good there also comes the bad, and so Kelly is learning to be choosy. "We get a steady stream of stuff about the college," he explains, and while the materials are always appreciated, they are not always relevant or necessary. "We're getting much more serious about building collections that directly support teaching and research."

The Kim-Wait/Eisenberg Native American Literature Collection

As such, Kelly is especially excited about one of the newest acquisitions for the Archives, the Kim-Wait/Eisenberg Native American Literature Collection. In August 2013, two new faculty members were hired to teach Native American Studies at Amherst. At the time, it so happened a major collection of books by Native American authors had gone up for sale, piquing Kelly's interest. Kelly approached the new faculty members to gauge their interest in the collection, which was high, and eventually word got around. With help from Amherst alum Younghee Kim-Wait in the form of a six-figure cash gift, it was soon made possible for the Archives to purchase the Native American collection. "This is how I want everything to happen from now on," Kelly daydreams, thinking it like a perfect storm of acquisitions. The collection includes fiction, poetry, history, philosophy, sermons, anthropological works, photography, activism, books for children, and much more, with items dating as far back as the 18th century alongside modern work from the likes of Sherman Alexie and Louise Erdrich. The result? "In my twenty years as a rare book librarian, I've never seen the books fly off the shelves like this."

Endowments and Acquisition Funds

Archives & Special Collections doesn't have to rely solely on donations, however, as Kelly counts about a dozen different endowments at his disposal. "About a quarter of them have serious restrictions," he says, citing one endowed fund that is reserved for the acquisition of 18th century books only. Others are completely unrestricted. "If we ever really need something, we could make a request from Acquisitions," with Kelly adding that he is always negotiating for acquisitions, and always negotiating with that in mind. He estimates that the dozen or so endowments collectively cover between $120,000 and $175,000, depending on the markets.

Frost Library, as a whole, is still buying as many books as ever. "There's a slight tip toward electronic," Kelly says, "but the library is still dedicated to print." Buying in

Archives & Special Collections, however, typically fluctuates with how well the funds produce each year. But with the collection's renewed mission statement, Kelly also wants to establish a certain foothold in the library community's mind: when it comes to asking for books, ask Archives & Special Collections. "Especially this past year, people have started to realize we have money to spend." He recalls an Asian Studies professor who had come to him with an unsure request for a book on Japanese photography. "The book was five hundred dollars, and [the professor] didn't know if we'd be able to get it." Archives & Special Collections was happy to oblige and quickly acquired the book. It is a balancing act, but Kelly welcomes faculty to approach the Archives in this manner with such requests—all to support the teaching and research of Amherst College.

Digitization

Full-Speed Ahead

Three years ago, a three-way campus partnership between Frost Library, Information Technology Services, and the Digital Programs Department resulted in the establishment of Amherst College Digital Collections (ACDC), a repository holding tens of thousands of digitized art works, photographs, manuscripts, books, and other media. As with most academic libraries these days, the retirement of Amherst's slide librarian created the space for such a digital programs position. "We're moving full-speed ahead with digital initiatives," reports Kelly. "Half of [ACDC's] focus was serving what the slide library did, but they're also moving us into the digital realm," focusing on digitizing rare and unique collections from the Archives.

The first order of business was to digitize the Emily Dickinson collection. As Kelly notes, Amherst is "kind of out of the way" and is not located in a major metropolitan area. "So we're trying to digitize the things that would be most useful to scholarship." The decision to start with the Dickinson collection was an obvious one as Dickinson is nearly synonymous with Amherst and demand for such materials is always high. Of course, digitization of these manuscripts saves significant wear and tear on the artifacts.

"We're focusing on unique things," Kelly goes on. "We try to think, 'What don't people expect to find at Amherst?' and the Alumni Relations people love us for that." This includes anything from Medieval manuscripts to Walt Whitman manuscripts, although due to copyright issues the focus is mostly on 19th century materials. "We want to appeal to the wide world of scholars, as well as the general public, and Amherst faculty and students." Other digitization projects of note include a missionary diary detailing eyewitness accounts of genocide from 1866 to 1906 as well as all of Edward Hitchcock's notes and papers. The department is dedicated to open access, and as such the repository—which can be found at https://acdc.amherst.edu—is completely open to students, faculty, and the general public alike.

In-House Digitization

Much of the digitization work for the Archives & Special Collections is done in-house, and as the Digital Programs Department is also located on A-level in Frost Library, in-house is conveniently in-*hall*. "Everything has worked out beautifully," says Kelly, adding that, most importantly, nothing has been destroyed by digitization. Occasionally projects are outsourced, although these instances are more often the products of time constraints rather than a lack of resources: "[Archives & Special Collections] recently sent all of our yearbooks to a third party to digitize, but it was not because they were doing something that Amherst couldn't do." There is one project, however, that Kelly notes had to be sent to the Northeast Document Conservation Center (NEDCC), the nation's first independent conservation laboratory specializing in treating collections made of paper or parchment. The work was on a bound Persian manuscript. "We needed them to take it apart, digitize it, and re-bind it, and this is something that was just beyond [our] capabilities." The cost for such tedious and meticulous work was $20,000.

Outreach and Publicity

The Consecrated Eminence

With a staff too small to maintain multiple social media presences, the online presence of the Archives & Special Collections is focused almost entirely on its blog, *The Consecrated Eminence* (www.consecratedeminence.wordpress.com). Started in 2011, *The Consecrated Eminence*—whose title is an early nickname for Amherst College—relates news and updates concerning acquisitions at the Archives, digitization efforts, and other points of interest. The blog is updated weekly by a member of the staff. "So among the six of us, each one is responsible for a blog post every six weeks," Kelly says. Sometimes these posts will get re-posted via Amherst College's official Facebook page, or else re-tweeted by Frost Library's Twitter feed, as Kelly says the Archives adheres to the A.E.I.O.U. approach to digital marketing: Already Existing Information Optimally Uploaded.

Other Outreach Efforts

Kelly is also an active lecturer, and he very much sees a need for this kind of outreach as a counterpoint to the blog. "The blog is for alumni and students, faculty, the general public," he says, but at conferences he can interact with librarians, archivists, and other special collection professionals. This kind of sharing of ideas is essential to building and maintaining a relevant collection. Among other appointments, Kelly is due to speak at the North American and Indigenous Studies Association (NAISA) conference at the University of Texas at Austin at the end of May 2014, this of course in support of the Kim-Wait/Eisenberg Native American collection, a collection he looks to continue to build.

Exhibits

Student Curators

Perhaps one of the greatest successes the Archives has had with outreach, however, has been with its student-led exhibits. "We have at least one student-curated exhibit each year," says Kelly, explaining how some faculty have particularly latched onto this project as it presents an interesting exercise in writing. "It's not writing a five-page paper. It's writing five sentences on a card instead." This fall, students participating in the seminar *Shakespeare and the History of Books* will curate an exhibit, in conjunction with the class, to be displayed in Frost Library. Exhibits such as this one are not only informative and historical but are also, in many ways, a direct manifestation of the renewed mission of the Archives, reinforcing the collection as both a cultural arts and research center and a training ground for students.

Exhibit Space and Schedule

A renovation to Frost Library in the mid-1990s (and to the current facility of the Archives) gifted the Archives with "wonderful, amazing exhibit cases." What's more, in a recent renovation of the public area on the first floor, Archives & Special Collections was granted two more exhibit cases. Some of these spaces are accessible only when the Archives is accessible, while other exhibit spaces are available during open library hours. "We try to do two to three major installments a year," Kelly says, "but we're super flexible about it." The manageable space allotted to the Archives allows the department to adapt quickly, as Kelly relays they only have about the next two exhibits in the schedule planned.

Popular past exhibits have included a prominent ornithology exhibit as well as an exhibit showcasing the newly-acquired Native American collection—the ability to promote an acquisition quickly is a clear benefit of the scheduling flexibility afforded Kelly. The Archives also works with the fine art and natural history museums on campus, including the Beneski Museum of Natural History, located in a building less than a decade old. The museum currently holds, among other things, Edward Hitchcock's fossils. Previously, an exhibit at Frost Library presenting the history of scientific illustration also coincided with related materials on display at the time at the natural history museum.

Security and Theft

Not a Concern

The remodel to the library in the mid-1990s brought the security system at Archives & Special Collections completely up to speed. "We have our own system," says Kelly, "so we have a separate alarm. Campus security is great. It's a small college, so everybody knows everybody, and we have good relationships with [campus security] so they know why we're special. We have the same security standards you would encounter at Harvard or Yale." For instance, there is always someone watching the reading room. The Archives has a vault, which is secured and alarmed, as well as stacks that are secured and alarmed. Overall, in regard to theft, Kelly says, "it's not an acute concern."

The Consortium

Five Colleges and Special Collections

Amherst College has long been a member of the Five Colleges consortium, partnering with local schools Hampshire College, Mount Holyoke College, Smith College, and the University of Massachusetts Amherst "to promote the broad educational and cultural objectives of its member institutions," as per the consortium's website. The consortium, which was established in 1965, naturally extends to the library and special collections, connecting the respective departments of the five schools in an effort to make use of shared resources and information. “About once a month there will be a meeting with the special collections folks from all five colleges,” says Kelly, and while they have yet to coordinate on any major exhibits, they have reached a point where these is a regular exchange of students. “So if we have students here looking at something,” explains Kelly, “we might send them over to Smith because [Smith] has a good collection of something in particular.” One prime example of consortium collaboration, however, is evident in the shared database that houses the finding aids across all five institutions. The Five College Archives and Manuscript Collection (5CAM) was a grant-funded project created about a dozen years ago that currently includes more than 700 findings aids, and growing. “Everyone has different strengths,” says Kelly. “So it’s good to have colleagues and to keep in touch.”

Printed in Great Britain
by Amazon

78944371R00045